Parks Canada Policy

For more information contact:
Parks Canada, 10 Wellington Street,
Hull, Que. K1A 0H4; or
Parks Canada regional offices:

Calgary
134-11th Ave. South East, Calgary, Alta.
T2G 0X5
Phone (403) 231-4401

Winnipeg
114 Garry Street, Winnipeg, Man.
R3C 1G1
Phone (204) 985-2110

Cornwall
132 Second Street East, Cornwall, Ont.
K6H 5V4
Phone (613) 933-7951

Quebec
1141 Route de l'Eglise, Ste-Foy, Que.
G1V 4H5
Phone (418) 694-4177

Halifax
Historic Properties, Upper Water Street,
Halifax, N.S. B3J 1S9
Phone (902) 426-3436

Preface

As Canadians, we have a justifiable pride in the beauty of our natural landscapes and in the history of our nation. Parks Canada is the federal agency whose clear mandate is to protect outstanding natural areas and historic places of Canadian significance across the country. As such, Parks Canada's activities play a vital role in the preservation of our national heritage for present and future generations.

Federal initiatives have evolved considerably since the establishment of our first national park in Banff in 1885. Our activities now encompass a system of national parks in every province and territory, national historic parks and sites representing a broad range of historic themes, heritage canals in eastern Canada, and joint Agreements for Recreation and Conservation with several provinces. In addition, new initiatives to protect other aspects of our natural and cultural heritage are underway — Canadian landmarks, Canadian heritage rivers and heritage buildings. Taken together, these activities comprise the Parks Canada program.

I am pleased to introduce this statement of the Government of Canada's policies which will guide the future direction of the Parks Canada program. It is the result of consultations with federal departments and agencies, provincial and territorial governments, hundreds of non-governmental organizations and interested individuals. Their efforts in developing and refining this policy reflect a deep-seated concern for the protection of Canada's heritage and a widespread public appreciation of its value to all Canadians.

I am particularly excited by the progress that has been made toward the establishment of a Canadian system of heritage rivers. I believe that wild, scenic and historic rivers are important but neglected aspects of our heritage. The policies for this and other new initiatives outlined herein will be elaborated after further consultations with the provinces and territories.

National parks, national historic parks and the other elements of the Parks Canada system provide significant opportunities for us to learn about our heritage, to enjoy outdoor activities and to develop our tourism industry for which these special places are a focus. Equally important, they are an act of faith in the future of Canda: by preserving wilderness tracts and historic resources we are asserting our collective belief that there are special places whose importance transcends their immediate contribution to our gross national product. This is a responsibility not only to future generations of Canadians but also to all mankind as part of international heritage efforts.

As Minister responsible for Parks Canada, I commit myself and my department to the implementation of these policies. But no matter how enlightened policies are, and how wisely they are employed, constant and enthusiastic public support will always be crucial to the protection of Canada's natural and cultural heritage.

J. Hugh Faulkner
Minister responsible for Parks Canada

Table of Contents

Introduction

Evolution of Policy

The Parks Canada program is based on the conviction that places of natural and cultural significance constitute a national inheritance which should be protected.

In 1885 the federal government set aside a 10-square-mile area of the Rocky Mountains, including the Banff hot springs. This was the beginning of Canada's system of national parks. Even in these early years federal policy affirmed that these outstanding scenic resources should be publicly owned. The Rocky Mountains Parks Act of 1887 stated that the area was reserved as "a public park and pleasure ground for the benefit, advantage and enjoyment of the people of Canada".

In 1917, Fort Anne became the first National Historic Park when it was transferred from the jurisdiction of the Department of the Militia to the Dominion Parks Branch. In 1919, the federal government set up the Historic Sites and Monuments Board of Canada to advise the Minister concerning the national historic significance of persons, places or events. Since then the federal government has administered historic and natural parks as a single program emphasizing the common themes of national inheritance and public ownership.

In 1930 Parliament approved the National Parks Act. The Act provided legislative protection for national park lands and clarified that these places were to be used by the public so as to leave them unimpaired.

Section 4 of the 1930 Act stated:
"The Parks are hereby dedicated to the people of Canada for their benefit, education and enjoyment, subject to the provisions of this Act and the Regulations, and such Parks shall be maintained and made use of so as to leave them unimpaired for the enjoyment of future generations."

In 1953 the Historic Sites and Monuments Act was passed. This Act formally established the Historic Sites and Monuments Board as an advisory body to the Minister and gave the Minister statutory responsibility for developing and implementing a national program commemorating persons, places and events of prime national historic and prehistoric interest.

In the 1960's Canadians became more aware of their natural environment and developed a renewed interest in their history. The number of visitors to national and historic parks increased sharply leading to a growing concern about park protection and appropriate use. As a result, policies were prepared and issued for national parks in 1964 and national historic sites in 1967. These policies reflected changing times; greater emphasis was placed on protection of natural and historic resources, interpretation and educational activities, and professional planning.

Need for a New Policy

Since the 1964 and 1967 policies were published there has been a rapid expansion of the traditional activities of national parks and national historic parks and sites. The amount of land within the national parks system has more than doubled to include areas in every province and both territories. The number, scope and complexity of national historic parks and sites have also increased.

Increases in the numbers of parks and sites are not the only changes. The responsibility for certain historic canals was transferred from the Ministry of Transport to the National and Historic Parks Branch in recognition of the fact that their primary importance had shifted from their use as commercial routes to their status as historic and recreational resources. Also, a series of new initiatives was proposed in the 1972 publication "Byways and Special Places" -- national landmarks, heritage rivers, national marine parks, historic land trails, historic waterways and scenic and historic parkways.

Other new activities arose from a new perception of the importance of our cultural as well as our natural heritage: the launching of Heritage Canada, the Canadian Inventory of Historic Buildings, and, most recently, the proposed Canadian Register of Heritage Property. These initiatives represent a desire to find new and flexible ways of identifying, protecting and presenting heritage resources.

Many Canadians now regard places of natural or historic significance not just as isolated monuments or scenic places to be preserved but as a means of learning about, and understanding the evolution of natural and historic environments. One of the most important challenges facing Parks Canada is to accommodate these new directions in its policies.

Parks Canada's policies must also be seen in the light of changing capabilities and priorities of federal, provincial and territorial governments. The federal role requires clarification particularly as it relates to provincial and territorial responsibilities for outdoor recreation and heritage conservation, so that complementary and co-operative programs can be developed among all government agencies.

Recent international developments also have implications for Parks Canada's policies. Canadians are beginning to appreciate that protecting heritage resources is part of their international responsibility.

The Purposes and Structure of the New Policy

The main purpose of the new Parks Canada policy is to provide an integrated and comprehensive statement of broad principles to serve as a guide for future initiatives and for more detailed policy statements on specific areas. As such, the policy contains both revised versions of existing, now separate policies, as well as a number of new policies, set within the context of an overall program objective. A further purpose of producing a program policy for Parks Canada is to provide other agencies and the public with a consolidated statement of overall objectives for the program as a whole and for individual activities within it.

This document is divided into three parts: program policies, policies for Parks Canada's current activities, and policies for new initiatives. The first part is an overall policy for the Parks Canada program -- the objective and broad common principles underlying existing and future Parks Canada activities.

In the second part, a policy has been developed for each of the current activities in the Parks Canada

program. Each activity is regarded as an independent means of achieving the overall program objective. Thus, policies for the traditional activities of national parks and national historic parks and sites have been revised to meet current and foreseen needs and to illustrate their contribution to the overall Parks Canada objective. In addition, separate policy statements for historic parks and historic sites have been introduced. Policies for heritage canals and agreements for recreation and conservation (ARC) are included in Part II as well. In general the policies in Part II are not new but revised versions confirming recent Parks Canada actions and approaches.

These activity policies offer guidance for planning and managing each park. They also provide the framework for the development of more specific and more detailed policies which will guide the day-to-day efforts of Parks Canada personnel. Thus the broad policies contained in this document will be further elaborated through strategic policies in a number of key areas as required.

The third part includes discussion of the policy directions for three new Parks Canada initiatives: Canadian landmarks, Canadian heritage rivers and heritage buildings. In contrast to the activity policies in Part II, the policies for these new initiatives are evolving and will be finalized following discussions with provincial and territorial governments.

Part I
Parks Canada Program
Policy

Program Objective

Program Policies

Figure 1:
A mule deer in velvet, n.d.

Parks Canada Photo Library
Anonymous photographer

Figure 2:
Prince Edward Island National Park, n.d.

Parks Canada Photo Library
Anonymous photographer

Figure 3:
Spruce galls along the trail, in
Prince Edward Island National Park

Parks Canada Photo Library
Anonymous photographer

Figure 4:
A warm summer day atop the casemates of
the King's Bastion, Louisbourg National
Historic Park, 1924

Parks Canada Research Division
Anonymous photographer

Figure 5:
Paradise Valley Alpine Club of Canada, 1907

Courtesy of:
The Peter Whyte Foundation, Archives of the
Canadian Rockies, Banff Alberta.
The Byron Harmon Collection

Program Objective
To protect for all time those places which are significant examples of Canada's natural and cultural heritage and also to encourage public understanding, appreciation and enjoyment of this heritage in ways which leave it unimpaired for future generations.

The word "heritage" means an inheritance or a legacy; things of value which have been passed from one generation to the next.

What is the Canadian heritage we all share? We share our natural surroundings -- the prairies, the forests, the lakes, the mountains, the coastlines, the tundra with their variety of plants and wildlife. We also share a history -- from prehistoric man, Indian and Inuit cultures, early exploration and settlement by Europeans, the founding of the nation up to yesterday's events.

Certain places representative of Canada's natural and cultural heritage are of importance to all Canadians. These special places should be given the highest degree of protection and managed for the benefit of all Canadians within a national system so as to leave them unimpaired for future generations. Parks Canada, through the Parliament of Canada, is charged with this responsibility. Such places provide benchmarks to assist Canadians to know and appreciate their country and its cultures; to reinforce national unity through an appreciation of the diversity of Canada and its people; and, to enjoy opportunities for education, recreation and inspiration.

Program Policies

1.0
Protecting Heritage Resources

1.1
Protecting Natural and Cultural Resources
Parks Canada will make protection of heritage resources its primary consideration.

Ecological and historical integrity are Parks Canada's first considerations and must be regarded as prerequisites to use. Protection of heritage resources is fundamental to their use and enjoyment by present and future generations.

The various factors which contribute to deterioration of heritage resources will be analyzed by means of thorough research and protection will be offered in ways appropriate for the type, significance and sensitivity of the resources. Parks Canada recognizes a responsibility to encourage public understanding and enjoyment of heritage resources. The means of doing so in a particular situation will depend upon the constraints which are necessary to ensure the perpetuation and protection of such resources.

1.2
Impact Assessment and Review
Parks Canada will take into account, in its planning and management, the full range of implications of any proposed actions on public lands under its administration, management and control.

The consequences of any proposed project, program or activity under Parks Canada's management and control or on lands under its jurisdiction must be considered as early as possible in planning, and this assessment incorporated in the decision to proceed with, reject or modify the proposed action. Consideration should be given to the full range of possible adverse impacts: biophysical, Socio-economic, cultural, archaeological, historical and aesthetic. All actions with environmental implications are subjected to identification, measurement and evaluation procedures to the degree dictated by the magnitude of the potential for adverse effects. In this way, Parks Canada adheres to the Federal Environmental Assessment and Review Process established by Cabinet in 1973.

1.3
Identifying Heritage Resources
Parks Canada will identify, in consultation with provincial and territorial governments, heritage resources that are of national significance for possible inclusion in the Parks Canada system.

Parks Canada will undertake studies and inventories of Canada's heritage resources. Using criteria outlined in each activity policy, heritage resources of national significance will be identified and specific examples will be selected for possible establishment as elements in the Parks Canada system. Consultation with provincial and territorial governments is essential in park identification and selection.

1.4
Man/Land Relationships
Parks Canada will protect and present heritage resources in the Parks Canada system in ways which reflect the interrelationships between man and nature.

A distinction is sometimes made between places which are of cultural heritage significance, and places of natural heritage significance. But man and his environment cannot be separated. Parks Canada's efforts to preserve and present natural areas should not ignore the ways in which man has lived within a particular environment and efforts to protect and present historic places should recognize that physiography and climate have been significant factors in Canada's development and history.

1.5
Research
Parks Canada will conduct and encourage research for the identification, protection, understanding and use of Canada's heritage resources.

Research is essential for an understanding of heritage resources so that they can be identified, selected, protected, enjoyed and presented in a responsible and effective manner. Identification and selection of heritage resources of Canadian significance requires intensive studies and inventories of natural regions and historic themes. Protection of heritage resources requires continuing research into the impact of use and techniques of conservation and resource management. Meeting public needs often requires surveys and analyses to identify these needs and to determine how best to respond to them. Accurate interpretation programs must be based on competent research. In satisfying research requirements, Parks Canada will draw upon the expertise of researchers in federal, provincial and territorial government agencies, in universities and in the private sector, as well as upon the knowledge and experience of individual citizens.

In addition to undertaking essential research for

park management purposes, Parks Canada will encourage basic research which may expand man's knowledge of his world and which requires study of natural or cultural resources protected in the Parks Canada system.

The time, place and nature of research activities will be regulated to ensure the protection of heritage resources and the safety and enjoyment of the public. Research information will be made available to the public.

2.0
Public Understanding, Appreciation and Enjoyment

2.1
Information and Interpretation
Parks Canada will undertake a variety of information and interpretation programs to encourage public understanding and appropriate use of heritage resources.

There are three elements in Parks Canada's information and interpretation activities. Parks Canada will inform the general public of its programs, activities, policies, plans and management practices. It will also undertake interpretation programs within parks and through extension programs to illustrate the meaning and value of heritage resources. Thirdly, Parks Canada will provide information to make visitors aware of opportunities for the enjoyment of heritage resources.

2.2
Public Participation
Parks Canada will provide opportunities for public participation at national, regional and local levels, in the development of policies and plans.

Parks Canada is committed to the principle of public participation and will encourage it to the fullest extent possible. The ultimate responsibility for policies and plans and their implementation rests with the Minister responsible for Parks Canada.

Public participation presents numerous advantages. It allows people interested in heritage issues to meet and exchange information and points of view. Citizens' ideas and comments can provide valuable input to the policy making and planning process. Public input becomes an integral part of this process and results in better decisions. Through such participation, there can be a better understanding of the objectives of Parks Canada and increased public support essential for heritage protection.

Parks Canada protects places which are the heritage of all Canadians. All interested Canadians, therefore, will be invited to state their views on such major issues as national policies, new park establishment, park management plans and large new development proposals. In addition, opportunities for public participation will be provided to those at the local and regional level who have special concerns because they are more directly affected by Parks Canada's activities and operations.

There is no single public participation mechanism suitable to every situation. Therefore opportunities for public participation will be provided in a variety of ways: public information meetings, workshops, questionnaires, interviews, public hearings, seminars, publications, or advisory committees. The approach followed will vary according to the nature and scope of the issues being discussed. For certain matters such as the preparation of management plans, a consistent general approach will be followed for national parks across the country, as outlined in the National Parks Policy. In addition, Parks Canada staff are available to discuss comments and suggestions from organizations and individuals.

For public participation to be effective, certain principles are fundamental:
• public discussion prior to final decisions;
• clear and accurate information;
• indication of areas requiring decisions and relevant policies, legislation and agreements;
• adequate notice and time for public review;
• careful consideration of public input;
• information on the nature of comments received and on Parks Canada's response to participants.

Besides participating in the development of policies and plans, there are other ways in which the public can become involved in the Parks Canada program. For example, there is an increasing desire on the part of individuals and local non-profit organizations to volunteer their services to assist in interpretation or other park operations. Various co-operative arrangements may be possible with organizations and individuals on matters such as research and public information. Policies have been developed to encourage and facilitate volunteer efforts and co-operative activities.

2.3
Outdoor Recreation
Parks Canada will provide opportunities for outdoor recreation within the Parks Canada system as means for present and future generations to understand and

enjoy heritage resources in ways consistent with protection of these resources.

Parks Canada's primary concern is to protect and present heritage resources of national significance. Thus public demand for outdoor recreation opportunities in a particular locality is not justification for Parks Canada's participation. Provincial and territorial governments and their agencies, however, have a specific mandate for recreation. Private organizations and individuals also play a role in meeting these demands.

Certain outdoor recreation activities offer a valuable means for enjoying and understanding heritage resources. Parks Canada will encourage those outdoor recreation uses which are directly associated with, and dependent on, heritage resources subject to requirements for resource protection, visitor safety and protection of the rights of other visitors. Within these constraints a variety of activities will be offered in different seasons.

Parks Canada can fulfil only some of the recreation needs of Canadians. Other needs can be met in places which do not have national heritage significance. Provincial, territorial, municipal and private agencies will be encouraged to develop complementary recreation activities and facilities.

2.4
Facilities and Services
Parks Canada will ensure that those facilities and services which are essential and appropriate for public access, understanding and enjoyment are provided and maintained to an appropriate standard.

Certain facilities and services are essential for public access, understanding and enjoyment of elements in the Parks Canada system. The type, location, scale, design and means by which such facilities and services are provided will reflect the particular circumstances. For example, consideration will be given to materials, energy conservation and architectural motif. Facilities and services may be provided by Parks Canada or by contract with private enterprise. The level of service and the quality of facilities will be maintained to standards set by Parks Canada.

2.5
Finance
Parks Canada will finance its activities from that portion of federal tax revenues allocated to it by the Parliament of Canada, may charge fees for specific services, and under certain circumstances may receive gifts or donations in order to meet its objective.

Since 1885, the federal government has accepted that protection and presentation of the Canadian heritage is a worthwhile investment for present and future generations of Canadians. Therefore, Parks Canada is financed by federal tax revenues allocated to it by the Parliament of Canada.

Fees may be charged for services such as the use of certain facilities, motor vehicle access, publications, concession privileges and land uses. Such fees will reflect the need for the federal treasury to recover a portion of the costs of operation and maintenance but will not be so high as to discourage public enjoyment of heritage resources.

Canadians and others may wish to contribute to the protection of their heritage by donating monies, lands or objects to Parks Canada. Such gifts or donations will be accepted providing their use furthers the work of the program for the benefit of all Canadians.

3.0
Roles and Relationships

3.1
Federal Context
Parks Canada will take the lead role in federal government activities related to protecting and presenting places representative of Canada's natural and cultural heritage and will carry out its mandate in close co-operation with related federal agencies.

Parks Canada is the federal agency concerned with places of national heritage significance. Many of its activities are closely related to those of other federal agencies. Some have the primary federal responsibility for various aspects of Canada's heritage such as museum objects, archaeology, the arts, archival material or endangered species. In addition others have objectives which relate indirectly to the mandate of Parks Canada, such as tourism, regional economic development, public works, broadcasting, film, fitness and amateur sport. All of the agencies involved in these activities share with Parks Canada a common concern with the achievement of Canada's heritage objectives, and this common concern will be expressed through close cooperation and consultations between them and Parks Canada. Their interests and responsibilities will be considered by interdepartmental committees and consultation on specific matters of mutual concern. Some activities are currently coordinated through committees such as the Federal Advisory and Co-ordinating Committee on Heritage Conservation (FACCHC) and the Interdepartmental Committee on Tourism. Parks Canada can provide advice and assistance on matters calling for its special expertise, and can encourage others to consider heritage protection in the implementation of their ongoing programs. In some cases, Parks Canada will rely upon the expertise of other federal agencies in carrying out its programs.

3.2
Federal-Provincial Relations
Parks Canada will fulfil its mandate in ways that recognize provincial and territorial responsibilities and complement their efforts in related fields.

Parks Canada is responsible for the protection and the presentation of places representative of Canada's natural and cultural heritage. Provinces have responsibilities in many related areas such as natural resources, education, culture, provincial parks and recreation.

Parks Canada will continue to actively seek provincial and territorial agreement and support for its national program in the interest of all Canadians. For example, Parks Canada will enter into agreements for recreation and conservation (ARC) with provinces to enable joint action in certain heritage areas. New initiatives proposed in this policy, such as Canadian landmarks and Canadian heritage rivers, are based on a flexible approach whereby provincially and federally protected areas together comprise a Canadian system. Federal-provincial agreements are required prior to the establishment of new national parks because the administration and control of most Crown lands is vested in the provinces.

To avoid duplication and to ensure that limited funds and staff are applied where they are most needed, close coordination of federal, provincial and territorial programs is necessary. Various mechanisms are available such as Parks Canada's five regional offices, annual federal/provincial conferences and increasingly, senior consultative committees between Parks Canada and individual provinces. Parks Canada can also serve as a contact point for provincial governments to help resolve specific issues arising where various other federal programs have an impact on provincial parks and heritage conservation activities.

3.3
Regional Integration
Parks Canada will seek to integrate elements of the Parks Canada system with surrounding regions so as to have a positive social, economic and physical impact.

Parks Canada is aware of the potential impact of its actions, both positive and negative, on adjacent areas. Economic development and local employment result directly and indirectly from park establishment and operation. Inevitably there are social consequences, particularly when traditional land uses and employment are affected or when large numbers of visitors are attracted to a particular location. There may be physical impacts as a result of facilities provided for visitors or actions required to protect heritage resources.

Concern for the impact of its actions does not imply that Parks Canada is primarily a program of regional social or economic development. By acting in a manner sensitive to local concerns and in close collaboration with other government agencies Parks Canada will strive to fulfill its mandate in ways which will be beneficial to, and ensure the best possible integration with, surrounding regions. Local communities and citizens cannot be asked to bear a disproportionate share of the costs of protecting and presenting the national heritage of all Canadians. Therefore, Parks Canada will co-operate with provincial and territorial agencies and, through them, with municipalities responsible for planning surrounding areas so as to resolve social, economic and physical impacts in a fashion compatible with Parks Canada's objectives. In certain cases, financial assistance may be provided for the development of municipal infrastructure necessary to encourage tourism developments outside parks, by means of federal-provincial cost-sharing agreements through other federal agencies.

3.4
International Role
Parks Canada will assume a leading role in fulfilling Canada's international responsibilities for the protection and presentation of places representative of the world's natural and cultural heritage.

Parks Canada's work is part of a worldwide endeavour to protect and present aspects of the heritage shared with all mankind.

Parks Canada participates in a number of international organizations concerned with protection of the natural and cultural heritage including the International Union for the Conservation of Nature and Natural Resources (IUCN), the International Council for Monuments and Sites (ICOMOS), and the International Centre for the Study of Preservation and Restoration of Cultural Property (The Rome Centre).

In 1976 Canada acceded to the World Heritage Convention, a UNESCO convention providing for the protection of the world cultural and natural heritage.

Parks Canada has been designated as the primary agency responsible for fulfilling Canada's obligations under this convention.

Under the UNESCO Man and the Biosphere Program, protected areas known as Biosphere Reserves are being created in many countries to conserve the diversity and integrity of plant and animal communities within natural ecosystems. Certain sites within selected Canadian national parks may be designated as core areas of Biosphere Reserves.

Canada has much to learn from other nations and, in turn, can offer valuable assistance. Under several bilateral agreements, Parks Canada undertakes exchanges of information and personnel and provides technical assistance to other countries. Also, Parks Canada has varying degrees of responsibility for certain natural and historic parks located along the Canada-U.S. Border.

Part II
Policies for Parks Canada
Activities

National Historic Sites
National Historic Parks
National Parks
Heritage Canals
Agreements for Recreation and Conservation

Figure 6:
Dedication Ceremony for the Cairn at
King's Bastion, Louisbourg National Historic Park,
Nova Scotia, August 1926.

Parks Canada Research Division
Anonymous photographer

Figure 7:
A view of the Gunpowder Magazine and
Officer's Barracks of Fort Anne National
Historic Park, n.d.

Parks Canada Research Division
Anonymous photographer

Figure 8:
Climbers on the summit horn of Mount Resplendent,
Mount Robson Alpine Club of Canada 1913.

Courtesy of:
The Peter Whyte Foundation, Archives of the
Canadian Rockies, Banff, Alberta.
The Byron Harmon Collection.

Figure 9:
A family outing in Kejimkujik
National Park, n.d.

Parks Canada Photo Library
Anonymous photographer

Figure 10:
The Camp at the Elbow of the North
Saskatchewan River, CPR Survey,
September 1871

Courtesy of:
The Public Archives of Canada
National Photography Collection
Charles Horetzky photographer

6

7

9

8

10

Figure 11:
Dedication Ceremony for the Cairn at
King's Bastion, Louisbourg National Historic Park,
Nova Scotia, August 1926

Parks Canada Research Division
Anonymous photographer

Background
One of the most effective ways to stimulate popular interest in, and understanding of, Canadian history is to focus attention to those specific locations most directly associated with historic persons, places or events.

Since 1923, the federal government has erected plaques or monuments to commemorate persons, places or events which are of national historic significance. Locations where such commemoration takes place are called national historic sites and there are now over 600 of them. In special cases, cost-sharing agreements may permit the commemoration and the protection of nationally significant historic structures.

Commemoration by a plaque or monument does not directly ensure the protection of historic resources but it does identify and afford formal recognition to the location and significance of certain aspects of Canadian history.

Parks Canada Objective for National Historic Sites
To encourage public understanding of Canada's historical heritage by commemorating persons, places and events of national historic significance with plaques, monuments or by other means funded by cost-sharing agreements.

1.0
Identifying Persons, Places and Events of National Historic Significance

Only those persons, places and events which are of historic significance on a national level will be commemorated by Parks Canada as national historic sites. The identification of persons, places and events of national historic significance is based on recommendations of the Historic Sites and Monuments Board of Canada which serves as an advisory body to the Minister responsible for Parks Canada. The Board is assisted by Parks Canada's staff through studies of broad historical themes and research on specific persons, places or events. In the case of prehistoric themes, Parks Canada works in close collaboration with archaeologists of the National Museum of Man.

1.1
Parks Canada will identify and undertake studies of the major themes of Canadian history and prehistory within which persons, places and events of national historic significance will be identified.

1.2
Parks Canada will undertake or encourage the compilation of inventories of prehistoric and historic resources related to certain themes of Canadian history to assist in identifying the historic significance of specific persons, places and events.

1.3
Parks Canada will undertake detailed research into historic significance of persons, places and events to assist the Historic Sites and Monuments Board of Canada.

1.4
Written submissions from the public to the Historic Sites and Monuments Board of Canada concerning persons, places and events which might qualify as being of national historic significance are welcomed.

1.5
The Historic Sites and Monuments Board of Canada receives written submissions, studies background research, and advises the Minister responsible for Parks Canada of those persons, places and events which it considers to be of national historic significance.

1.6
Persons, places and events of national historic significance will be identified according to the following general criteria:
i)persons who have had a significant impact on Canadian history irrespective of the country in which all or part of their achievements occurred; or
ii)events or movements which have shaped Canadian history or which illustrate effectively the broad cultural, social, political, economic, or military themes of Canadian history; or
iii)places which shed light on or illustrate effectively the culture of a prehistoric people, or are associated with important archaeological discoveries; or
iv)structures which embody the distinguishing characteristics of an architectural and engineering type exceptionally valuable for the study of a style or method of construction of its period or which are examples of the work of a master builder, designer, engineer or architect.

1.7
The following will not be eligible for consideration as being of national historic significance:
i)cemeteries and graves, except those of the Fathers of Confederation and those having archaeological significance;
ii)structures that have been moved from their original location;
iii)places outside Canada;
iv)living persons.

2.0
Commemoration at National Historic Sites

2.1
General Policies

2.1.1
Persons, places and events identified as being of national historic significance will be commemorated.

2.1.2
The Historic Sites and Monuments Board of Canada recommends to the Minister the appropriate form and location for commemoration in accordance with policies 2.2 and 2.3.

2.2
Location for Commemoration

2.2.1
Persons of national historic significance will be commemorated at a place within Canada which is closely associated with their contribution to Canadian history.

2.2.2
Events of national historic significance will be commemorated where they occurred.

2.2.3
The places at which persons, places and events of national historic significance are commemorated need not be owned by the federal government.

2.3
Forms of Commemoration

2.3.1
Plaques

2.3.1.1
The standard form of commemoration will be by means of a plaque.

2.3.1.2
The appropriate text for the inscription on a commemorative plaque will be recommended to the Minister by the Historic Sites and Monuments Board of Canada.

2.3.1.3
The text on all plaques will appear in both official languages and in other language(s) if appropriate.

2.3.1.4
The presence of a commemorative plaque at a place not owned by the federal government does not commit Parks Canada to protect or assist in the preservation of the place or any historic resources located thereon.

2.3.2
Monuments

2.3.2.1
Monuments may be erected to commemorate persons, places or events of exceptional importance in Canadian history.

2.3.2.2
The design of such monuments should convey to the public the theme to be emphasized in connection with the person, place or event.

2.3.2.3
Proposals for the design of distinctive monuments will be invited from artists of the particular region of Canada where the monument is to be erected.

2.3.3
Cost-Sharing Agreements

2.3.3.1
Parks Canada may provide financial and technical assistance to municipal and provincial governments as well as private non-profit organizations, e.g., local historical societies, to acquire and restore structures of national historic significance which deserve more than a commemorative plaque, but which do not warrant acquisition by Parks Canada as a national historic park.

2.3.3.2
Cost-sharing agreements will be considered:
i)where there are existing historic resources which are not adequately protected; and
ii)where there is a local organization which is willing to share the costs of acquisition and protection and to undertake continuing operation; and
iii)where the planned use of the preserved historic structure is appropriate.

2.4
Co-operation

2.4.1
Parks Canada will co-operate with provincial and territorial governments and other agencies responsible for commemorative historic plaques to avoid unnecessary duplication.

2.4.2
Parks Canada will co-operate with local, provincial and territorial governments and other interested groups, including local historical societies, in making arrangements for formal ceremonies to unveil a plaque or monument.

2.5
Information

2.5.1
Parks Canada will inform the public of the location and significance of national historic sites.

2.5.2
Research information on national historic sites will be made available to the public.

Figure 12:
Overlooking the waterfront from the Citadel at
Halifax Nova Scotia, c. 1860-70

Courtesy of:
The Public Archives of Canada
National Photography Collection
The Hastings Doyle Album, p. 12

Background

Historic resources in Canada are scarce, often unique, non-renewable, tangible relics of man's past. They range from archaeological evidence of man's earliest presence on this continent to recent architecture and technology; from archaeological and ethnographic specimens, through documents and antiques to buildings and large tracts of land. All are in some measure creations of the human mind and hands, illustrations from the past which, if preserved, will benefit present and future generations. They are easily destroyed and, once gone, can never be replaced.

Each year, some of Canada's historic resources are destroyed by natural causes such as erosion and age and it is probable that the destruction caused by man himself is even more serious. The demands of an industrial society and a growing population mean that historic resources are increasingly vulnerable.

The protection of historic resources in Canada is a responsibility which is shared by different levels of government and which can be accomplished in a variety of ways. Museums deal primarily with the collection, preservation and display of cultural objects, not with the acquisition and protection of actual sites. Historic parks focus directly on certain places in terms of their relevance to Canadian history, either by concentrating on one period or, sometimes, by illustrating historical evolution. Historic parks attempt to provide a realistic environment where historic resources can be seen in their natural and cultural context. Through the complementary efforts of historic museums and parks at national, provincial and local levels, the important historic resources of Canada can be protected and the many themes of Canadian history can be illustrated.

Provincial and territorial governments have important objectives for their cultural heritage resources. It is essential that Parks Canada be sensitive to provincial and territorial aims and activities in this area. Parks Canada will attempt to coordinate its efforts with related programs to avoid duplication and enable efficient use of resources. It will actively seek provincial and territorial support for the establishment of national historic parks.

National historic parks are the means by which outstanding historic resources of importance to all Canadians can be protected by the federal government and made accessible to the public in their original location and in an authentic setting. Three factors distinguish a national historic park:
• national historic significance;
• protection and interpretation at the original place and in an authentic setting; and
• establishment, protection, interpretation and management by the federal government.

Canada's national historic parks system began in 1917 with the establishment of Fort Anne as a national historic park. Since then many other national historic parks have been developed, particularly in the 1960's and 1970's, representing a variety of historical themes in locations across Canada.

Public interest in our history is evident from the large numbers of people who visit Canada's national historic parks each year. Lower Fort Garry, near Winnipeg, the Fortress of Louisbourg in Cape Breton, Dawson City in the Yukon, Fort Langley in British Columbia, les Forges du Saint-Maurice near Trois-Rivières and the Halifax Citadel are well-known examples of national historic parks.

And although national historic parks illustrate some of the themes of Canadian history, there is still much work to be done. For example, the early emphasis on military history is being balanced by attention to social and industrial themes. In fact, the system of national historic parks will never be complete, because each day we are living what will be history tomorrow.

There are many benefits of national historic parks. They serve as tangible and enduring reminders of the human heritage of Canada, and indicators of the achievements and lifestyle of our ancestors. By visiting the parks, Canadians can better understand and appreciate their past. Many people gain satisfaction from knowing that future generations will also be able to visit these areas. A growing number of Canadians are discovering that a visit to a national historic park is a pleasant and rewarding way to spend leisure time. The increased visitation, not only by Canadians but by visitors from other countries, may result in increased employment possibilities and tourism industry development in areas adjacent to national historic parks.

Parks Canada Objective for National Historic Parks

To protect for all time historic resources at places associated with persons, places and events of national historic significance in a system of national historic parks, and to encourage public understanding, appreciation and enjoyment of this historical heritage so as to leave it unimpaired for future generations.

1.0
The National Historic Parks System

Each of Canada's national historic parks illustrates an important part of the history of Canada. A system of national historic parks can underline the associations among different historic places, periods and themes and thereby encourage a deeper understanding of Canada's past.

Parks Canada strives to establish through co-operation with provincial and territorial governments such a system of national historic parks at locations across Canada where historic resources of national significance deserve protection and interpretation. The essential prerequisite for the establishment of a national historic park is the identification of persons, places and events of national historic significance, based on the recommendations of the Historic Sites and Monuments Board of Canada. This board serves as an advisory body to the Minister responsible for Parks Canada.

Most persons, places or events identified as of national historic significance will be commemorated by a plaque or monument at a national historic site. National historic parks, however, will only be established in certain circumstances to ensure that the system of national historic parks is of the highest quality and reflects a balance among historic themes and geographical regions.

1.1
Identifying Persons, Places and Events of National Historic Significance

Policies for the identification of persons, places and events of national historic significance are the same as in Section 1. under National Historic Sites Policy.

1.2
Selecting Potential National Historic Parks

1.2.1

Potential national historic parks will be selected by Parks Canada according to the following criteria:
i)The place will have been identified as being of national historic significance or as being prominently associated with persons or events of major national historic significance; and
ii)The place will possess integrity, will include the original site, and, ideally, at least some original materials and workmanship. Intangible elements such as feelings and associations may be important in judging the integrity of an historic place; and
iii)The place will be related to a theme of Canadian history which does not already have sufficient representation in the system of national historic parks; and
iv)The place will have excellent potential for illustrating Canadian history; and
v)The place will include significant authentic historic resources; and
vi)It will be possible to protect the historic resources, including their authentic environment within the lands available and at an acceptable cost.

1.2.2

In selecting potential national historic parks consideration will be given to:
i)the advice of the Historic Sites and Monuments Board of Canada as to the appropriate form of commemoration of a person, place or event of national historic significance; and
ii)the degree to which the historic resources are currently protected or threatened; and
iii)geographic balance of national historic parks throughout Canada; and
iv)the activities and capabilities of other public and private agencies responsible for preserving aspects of Canada's historic heritage; and
v)international criteria for the protection of historic resources.

1.2.3

Potential national historic parks will be selected in consultation with the provincial or territorial government.

1.3
Establishing National Historic Parks

1.3.1

Parks Canada will prepare and periodically update a long-range system plan to guide the priorities for establishment and development of national historic parks.

1.3.2

Parks Canada will acquire land, buildings and other historic resources required for the establishment of a new national historic park, by purchase, long-term lease or other agreement.

1.3.3

Parks Canada will consult with the provincial or territorial government prior to the establishment of a new national historic park.

1.3.4
Parks Canada will consult with the interested public concerning the establishment of a new national historic park.

1.3.5
Each new national historic park will be formally established under the National Parks Act.

2.0
Protecting Heritage Resources in National Historic Parks
Heritage resources in national historic parks may include historic structures, historic artifacts, the historic environment and, in certain cases, natural resources. In national historic parks, Parks Canada will attempt to create and maintain an authentic historic setting by preserving existing historic resources and, where necessary, by accurately restoring or reconstructing aspects essential to an understanding of the site's history.

Protection and interpretation of historic resources can be accomplished by three types of treatment:

• *Preservation*: measures designed to maintain the existing form, integrity and material of historic resources.

• *Restoration*: recovery of the historic form and details of historic resources by removing later additions and replacing the missing original elements as accurately as possible.

• *Reconstruction*: accurate reproduction of historic structures or objects.

2.1
Protection of Historic Resources

2.1.1
The preservation of historic resources in their existing form will always be given first consideration over restoration or reconstruction.

2.1.2
Parks Canada will assess the impact of its proposed actions on the prehistoric, historic and natural resources in national historic parks.

2.2
Documentation
Comprehensive records will be established and maintained in the form of a complete dossier for all historic resources (places, structures, objects) related to national historic parks.

2.3
Historic Structures
Historic structures are works of man, created to serve some human activity and are usually by nature or design immovable. Examples are buildings, dams, canals, bridges, fortifications, gardens and roads.

2.3.1
Preservation

2.3.1.1
An historic structure will be stabilized or maintained in its existing form:
i)when the structure, upon acquisition already possesses the integrity and authenticity required; or
ii)when restoration or reconstruction is required or desirable but, for reasons of cost or lack of sufficient data, must be postponed; or
iii)when the structure has been restored or reconstructed by Parks Canada and requires ongoing maintenance.

2.3.1.2
Modern techniques and devices (such as for fire, temperature and humidity control) may be used when essential to protect historic structures and objects, and to ensure visitor safety but should intrude as little as possible on the historic atmosphere.

2.3.2
Restoration

2.3.2.1
Full or partial restoration of historic structures will only be undertaken under the following conditions:
i)when it is essential for public understanding of the historical associations and appearance of the national historic park; and
ii)when the existing structure is in good condition and retains most of its original details; and
iii)when sufficient data exist to permit accurate restoration; and
iv)when the cost of restoration can be justified in relation to the historic significance and interpretive potential of the structure.

2.3.2.2
Restoration of structures will be undertaken in such a way that the original historical fabric is safeguarded.

2.3.2.3
Restored or replaced material will be accurately recorded but should be indistinguishable from the original in order to maintain a realistic historic environment.

2.3.2.4
Subject to the availability of data, structures will normally be restored to their most significant historic period but earlier or later components of the structure may be preserved if they are of historic or artistic merit and can be of value in interpreting the evolution of the structure.

2.3.3
Reconstruction

2.3.3.1
Reconstruction of a vanished historic structure will only be undertaken under the following conditions:
i)when reconstruction is essential to public understanding of the historical associations and appearance of the national historic park; and
ii)when no appropriate alternative action can create such public understanding; and
iii)when there are no significant preservable remains which will be obliterated by reconstruction; and
iv)when sufficient historical and architectural data exist to permit an authentic reconstruction; and
v)when the cost of reconstruction can be justified in relation to the historic significance and interpretive potential of the structure.

2.3.3.2
Reconstructed structures will be identified as such.

2.3.3.3
Reconstruction will be on the original sites except where foundations are of historical merit and cannot be incorporated into the reconstruction; in such cases reconstruction if necessary may be adjacent to the original foundations.

2.4
Historic Artifacts
An historic artifact is material modified by man to produce an object of artistic, utilitarian or symbolic significance, attributed to past culture.

2.4.1
Conservation
Historic artifacts will be properly recorded, given appropriate conservation treatment and stored, transported, handled and exhibited in ways which ensure their continued survival with minimum deterioration.

2.4.2
Restoration

2.4.2.1
An historic object may be fully or partially restored:
i)when sufficient data exist to permit accurate restoration; and

ii)when the object is necessary for an interpretive display but cannot be properly understood without restoration; or
iii)when restoration is necessary for the survival of the object.

2.4.2.2
Replacement material will be accurately recorded but should be indistinguishable from the original.

2.4.3
Reproduction

2.4.3.1
Artifacts may be reproduced:
i)when sufficient data exist to permit accurate reproduction; and
ii)when the object is essential for public understanding through interpretation of the park story; and
iii)when no original exists, or an original that may exist is unobtainable or too delicate or too valuable for the use intended.

2.4.3.2
Reproduced artifacts will be identified as such.

2.5
Historic Environment

2.5.1
Parks Canada will preserve or restore the environment of a national historic park to its authentic historic form with a minimum of modification to suit modern tastes.

2.5.2
Where possible the natural environment, including gardens and landscapes, will be restored and maintained to resemble the appropriate historic period, except as outlined in section 2.6.

2.5.3
Administrative and visitor facilities and services which are required within a national historic park will be located and designed so as to minimize their intrusion on the historic environment and will, where possible, be housed in historic buildings.

2.5.4
Buffer zones should be established adjacent to national historic parks by land purchase, easements, lease or local zoning to prevent intrusions into the historic scene.

2.5.5
Efforts will be made to ensure that park operations, visitor use, safety measures, interpretation and other services do not disturb the historic environment.

2.6
Natural Features

2.6.1
Natural features within national historic parks will be protected:
i) when they are of scientific, ecological or esthetic significance and/or interest to the public; and
ii) when serious disturbance to the authentic historic environment will not occur.

2.6.2
Significant natural features within national historic parks may be managed according to the appropriate policies for national landmarks.

3.0
Public Understanding, Appreciation and Enjoyment of National Historic Parks
National historic parks are one means of enabling Canadians to experience important aspects of their history in an original setting. Besides protecting heritage resources, Parks Canada has a responsibility to make visits to national historic parks enjoyable and educational and to foster awareness and appreciation of Canada's history. This can be accomplished by disseminating information about the location and importance of national historic parks; by interpreting historic resources and their wider significance to both visitors and non-visitors; by providing opportunities for visitor use; and by providing essential facilities and services.

3.1
Information and Interpretation

3.1.1
Accurate information about national historic parks and the opportunities which they provide will be made available to the general public and to park visitors.

3.1.2
The interpretation program for a national historic park will be based on the historical resources at the park and the themes of Canadian history which they illustrate.

3.1.3
Physical aspects of the historic environment may be restored or recreated as an interpretation tool (e.g., restoration or reconstruction of structures, use of period furnishings, restoration and maintenance of the appropriate natural landscape) within the policies for the protection of heritage resources outlined in Section 2.

3.1.4
Living historical interpretation such as guides in period costumes, role playing, authentic craft demonstrations, etc. may be undertaken:
i) when sufficient information is available to ensure accuracy; and
ii) when it is appropriate to and enhances the park story; and
iii) when the cost can be justified in relation to historic significance and interpretive potential.

3.1.5
National historic parks will be presented, wherever possible, as they actually existed rather than as "typical" examples.

3.1.6
Modern interpretation techniques may be used to give park visitors historical background, detail and perspective.

3.1.7
To ensure that interpretive programs and techniques keep up with evolving visitor interest and needs, research of visitor expectations and reactions will be conducted periodically at the park level.

3.1.8
Special interpretation programs may be developed to meet the needs of particular audiences such as school groups.

3.1.9
Where appropriate, aspects of the natural environment may be interpreted in terms of their historical association or their significance as natural features.

3.2
Visitor Use of National Historic Parks

3.2.1
The primary purpose of visitor use of national historic parks is to encourage an understanding and enjoyment of Canada's history and of historical resources.

3.2.2
Recreational activities which are inspired by the historical or natural features will be encouraged to the extent that they do not intrude unduly on the historic environment or jeopardize the protection and direct enjoyment of historic resources.

3.2.3
Access of visitors to particular parts of a national historic park may be limited to protect historic resources or to ensure visitor safety and enjoyment.

3.2.4
Special events staged in historic parks by outside organizations will be permitted when such events are closely related to the theme of the park, when they do not jeopardize the integrity of the historic or physical environment, and when they do not detract from public enjoyment of the park.

3.3
Visitor Services and Facilities

3.3.1
Parks Canada will provide directly or by concession those services and facilities which are essential to public enjoyment of a particular national historic park in ways which do not intrude upon the historic environment.

3.3.2
Food services may be provided within national historic parks:
i)when such services are part of the historic environment; or
ii)when such services are essential because no reasonable alternative exists outside the park, or because a visit to the park normally requires several hours.

3.3.3
Campgrounds will only be developed in national historic parks under exceptional circumstances such as:
i)when there are no campgrounds available in the vicinity; and
ii)when it is not feasible for other public or private agencies to develop campgrounds in the vicinity; and
iii)when there is adequate land within the national historic park to permit campground development without jeopardizing the historic or significant natural environment.

3.3.4
Permanent visitor accommodation facilities may be developed within certain national historic parks in exceptional circumstances:
i)where there are suitable restored or reconstructed buildings which are not essential for primary park purposes, such as park interpretation centres, or for visitor or administrative services; and
ii)where such visitor use is an additional means of enhancing visitor understanding of the historic environment.

4.0
Research
Research is the key to accuracy in all work related to national historic parks, from the initial determination of national historic significance to restoration of historic details and information in the park brochure. By undertaking historical research related to national historic parks, Parks Canada can achieve its own objectives and also contribute to Canada's national historiography.

4.1
Parks Canada will encourage and conduct that historical, architectural, archaeological and socio-economic research which contributes directly to the identification, protection, development, interpretation, planning and managing of historic resources within national historic parks.

4.2
Development at national historic parks will not normally take place until adequate research has been completed.

4.3
Actions which reduce the potential for future research on historic resources will be avoided whenever possible.

4.4
Use of park resources, research files and collections of artifacts by scholars is encouraged where it is compatible with visitor activities but it is not the intention of Parks Canada to establish permanent research centres in national historic parks.

4.5
Research information will be made available to the public and where appropriate, research activities on sites will be interpreted to enhance public understanding of historic resources.

4.6
Parks Canada will co-operate with and draw upon the research of historians, historical societies and historic resources agencies at the local, provincial, territorial and national levels and upon the knowledge of individual citizens.

5.0
Management Plans
The development and management of a national historic park will be based on a carefully conceived management plan which states how important historic resources are to be protected and outlines those opportunities that will be provided for visitors' understanding and enjoyment. This management

plan is the means of implementing Parks Canada's policies in national historic parks.

5.1
A management plan will be prepared to guide the development and management of each national historic park.

5.2
Interim management guidelines will be prepared shortly after the establishment of a national historic park to guide initial management and development and to ensure that future options are not prejudiced.

5.3
The management plan will contain a clear definition of the themes of Canadian history to be illustrated and the objectives of the particular national historic park.

5.4
In national historic parks with extensive land areas, it may be necessary, as part of the management plan, to prepare a zoning plan indicating the type of activities which are appropriate in different parts of the park.

5.5
Opportunities will be provided for the public to participate in the planning for national historic parks.

5.6
The management plan and changes thereto must be approved by the Minister responsible for Parks Canada.

5.7
Parks Canada will co-operate with other levels of government, private organizations and individuals responsible for such facilities as transportation and accommodation of visitors to ensure that national historic parks are integrated into the surrounding region so as to have a positive social, economic and physical impact.

National Parks

Figure 13:
Climbers silhouetted against the Yoho Glacier.
Upper Yoho Alpine Club of Canada 1914

Courtesy of:
The Peter Whyte Foundation, Archives of the
Canadian Rockies, Banff Alberta.
The Byron Harmon Collection.

Background

Canadians live in a land rich in natural beauty. The shores of three oceans, the Great Lakes, mountains, prairies, thousands of lakes and rivers, forest and tundra - these along with their flora and fauna are some of the natural treasures we have inherited.

For centuries this landscape was affected mainly by natural forces. But more recently, with the advent of an agricultural and then an industrial society, human activities have been altering the natural environment at an accelerating pace.

National parks are a means of preserving in a natural state areas which are representative of the major natural environments of Canada. They are special places which protect part of the heritage of all Canadians, now and in the future. They offer a range of opportunities to learn about and enjoy the natural environment. In order to enable the continued protection of these areas, it is necessary to ensure that visitor activities do not result in harmful changes to ecology or to the appearance of the landscape. To this end, zones are identified within each park which reflect the degree of resource protection required and the type and intensity of visitor use that is appropriate. In this way, a balance can be achieved between visitor use and wilderness preservation within each national park. In some parks in remote and sensitive natural regions, where large areas are required for ecological preservation and where man can experience nature on its own terms, only certain zones may be designated, so as to maintain the entire area in a wilderness state.

Not all national parks are the same. In remote or northern areas, potential national parks may be identified which are the homeland of people who have traditionally depended on the land and its resources for their survival. Their culture reflects this fundamental relationship. In certain cases, lands which have been traditionally used by native people are the subject of unresolved native land claims. If such areas are to be protected within the national parks system, they must be planned and managed in a way which reflects these special circumstances. An appropriate balance must be maintained between the rights of the public to understand and enjoy Canada's natural heritage, the rights of local people to continue certain traditional uses and the requirement to protect the wilderness of the area.

The first national park in Canada was established in 1885 to protect the newly discovered Banff Hot Springs for public use. The national park system now covers 1.3 percent of Canada's land mass, including areas in each province and territory. Although a variety of landscapes is now represented in Canada's national park system, certain elements are missing; for example, arctic and sub-arctic natural regions and prairie grassland. In addition, marine natural regions are not well represented in the national parks system. Although there are complex jurisdictional problems related to their establishment, policies for national marine parks will be developed. Decisive action is required while the opportunities exist if the heritage of the past is to be passed on to the future. The identification and protection of our important natural heritage areas cannot await or accommodate the advance of competing land uses. National parks are an investment in the future. Foresight in preserving such areas will bring many future rewards even if access is difficult today.

On the international level, Canada's national parks are an important component of a world-wide endeavour to protect outstanding natural areas. Within Canada, the national parks are part of a family of parks and wildlife areas administered by different levels of government and designed to serve various public needs. Within this Canadian family of parks, the national parks are distinct because they are natural areas of Canadian significance, because they are protected by federal legislation and because they are financed by and dedicated to all Canadians.

There are many benefits of national parks. Some are intangible such as the knowledge that future generations will be able to appreciate wilderness areas of untouched natural beauty. Others are more tangible, such as the enjoyment of visiting national parks across Canada. There are also benefits which can be measured in terms of jobs created and tourism industry development. Furthermore, national parks are ecological benchmarks for research into natural processes and into the relative effects of man on lands outside national parks. For all these reasons, Canada has a responsibility to protect these special places and to encourage public appreciation now and in the future.

Parks Canada Objective for National Parks
To protect for all time representative natural areas of Canadian significance in a system of national parks, and to encourage public understanding, appreciation and enjoyment of this natural heritage so as to leave it unimpaired for future generations.

1.0
The National Park System

National parks are intended to protect representative examples of the diversity of Canada's landscape and marine areas for the benefit of present and future generations. To this end, Parks Canada has divided Canada into 48 natural regions, of which 39 are terrestrial and 9 are marine. Each of these natural regions should be represented in the system of national parks. In order to achieve this goal, certain natural areas are identified within each natural region, which include the greatest diversity of natural themes (biologic, geologic, physiographic, geographic and oceanographic) and which are therefore representative of the natural region. These areas are referred to as "representative natural areas of Canadian significance". Potential national parks are selected from among the representative natural areas of Canadian significance.

Parks Canada cannot, however, protect all of the areas identified as being representative natural areas of Canadian significance. By working with the provinces and territories to establish and make public a register listing identified areas, Parks Canada hopes to encourage other public agencies and appropriate private organizations to work toward their protection.

Public interest and support as well as the co-operation of provincial and territorial governments is essential for the establishment of new national parks or the adjustment of existing park boundaries. Within the provinces, a federal-provincial agreement is necessary setting out the terms and conditions of transfer of administration and control of required lands from the province to the federal government. The process of establishment may take several years and includes joint discussions and feasibility studies by the federal and provincial governments; agreement on terms of establishment and park boundaries; public involvement; resolution of land-use conflicts including agreement on traditional land uses which may be permitted and other special measures to reduce the impact of a new national park on local occupants or users; land assembly; and amendments to the federal legislation under which national parks are established. When this last step has been taken, Parks Canada can formally plan for the protection of the area and for public enjoyment of the park's natural heritage resources.

The federal-provincial agreement to create a new national park is one of the most significant steps in the process of national park establishment. It is a joint agreement, and as such, commits two levels of government to a common objective: to protect the park area and encourage public understanding and enjoyment of the area both at the time the park is established and in the future. When national parks are created in conjunction with native land claims, for example in the northern wilderness areas, a special agreement will be necessary between Parks Canada and representatives of local native people to set up an agreed joint management regime for the park. Without the support and co-operation of the provinces, territories, native organizations and the general public, the federal government cannot meet its responsibility to protect the natural heritage of all Canadians.

1.1
Identifying Representative Natural Areas of Canadian Significance

1.1.1
Representative natural areas of Canadian significance will be identified within each land and water natural region of Canada according to the following criteria:
i) The area must portray the diverse geological, physiographical, oceanographical and biological themes of a natural region; and
ii) The area must have experienced minimum modification by man or, if significant modification has occurred, must have potential for restoration to a natural state.

1.1.2
Representative natural areas of Canadian significance will be identified in consultation with provincial and territorial governments, other federal agencies and with the interested public.

1.1.3
Representative natural areas of Canadian significance will be identified regardless of their current protected status or jurisdiction.

1.2
Selecting Potential National Parks

1.2.1
Potential national parks will be selected from among identified representative natural areas of Canadian significance according to the following criteria:
i) the area will be within a natural region which does not already have sufficient representation in the system of national parks; and

ii)the area will be of a size and configuration so as to:

a)include a definable ecological unit(s) whose long term protection is feasible; and

b)offer opportunities for public understanding and enjoyment; and,

c)result in minimum long term disruption of the social and economic life in the surrounding region; and

d)exclude existing permanent communities.

1.2.2

In selecting potential national parks consideration will be given to:

i)the existence of possible threats to the natural environment of the area; and

ii)competing land uses; and

iii)the geographic balance of national parks throughout Canada; and

iv)the location and objectives of other protected natural areas; and

v)international criteria for national parks.

1.2.3

Potential national parks will be selected in consultation with provincial and territorial governments, other federal agencies and with the interested public.

1.2.4

Adjustments to the boundaries of existing national parks will be determined according to the policies for selecting potential national parks.

1.3
Establishing New National Parks

1.3.1

Parks Canada will develop and keep up-to-date a plan for the system of national parks to assist in setting priorities for the establishment of new national parks.

1.3.2

Parks Canada in conjunction with the provincial or territorial government, will consult with local communities and the interested public prior to the establishment of a new national park or the adjustment of boundaries of an existing national park.

1.3.3

It is the policy of the Department of Indian and Northern Affairs to ensure that an inventory of the non-renewable natural resource potential of areas in the Yukon and Northwest Territories be compiled prior to their formal establishment as new national parks. The fundamental qualities of the area which

recommend it for national park status will be taken into account in any land use activities associated with compiling the inventory. Parks Canada will cooperate with other federal agencies responsible for carrying out such inventories.

1.3.4

Commercial exploration, extraction or development of natural resources which exists prior to the establishment of a new national park will be terminated before the park is formally established. Certain traditional uses will be permitted to continue as outlined in section 3.2.11.

1.3.5

Parks Canada will contribute toward the cost of special provisions to reduce the impact of park establishment on occupants or other users of lands acquired for a national park.

1.3.6

A variety of means will be used to ensure the maximum possible opportunities for local residents to find employment and business opportunities related to the management of national parks.

1.3.7

The government of Canada will own all land and resources within national parks.

1.3.8

Private lands and interests will normally be acquired by negotiated settlement except in cases where a negotiated settlement cannot be reached and when the lands are essential for park purposes. In such situations, expropriation will be used.

1.3.9

Co-operative arrangements will be sought with provincial, territorial and federal agencies to ensure compatible use and management of lands adjacent to the national park.

1.3.10

National parks will be formally established following amendment to the schedule to the National Parks Act by the Parliament of Canada.

1.3.11

National Parks within the provinces will be established according to an agreement between the Government of Canada and the provincial government setting out the terms for transfer of administration and control of required lands to the Crown in right of Canada. Parks Canada will share equally with the province the costs of acquiring private lands and interests.

1.3.12

National parks in the northern territories will be established after consultation with the territorial governments.

1.3.13

Where new national parks are established in conjunction with the settlement of land claims of native people, an agreement will be negotiated between Parks Canada and representatives of local native communities prior to formal establishment of the national park creating a joint management regime for the planning and management of the national park.

1.3.14

Boundaries of national parks would not be finally established in legislation until a settlement of relevant native claims is reached. As an interim measure such areas may be set aside as "national park reserves".

2.0

National Parks Zoning System

Zoning is one of the most important tools for the planning, development and management of national parks. The national parks zoning system is a resource-based approach by which land and water areas of a national park are classified according to their need for protection and their capability to accommodate visitors. It provides a guide for the activities of both visitors and managers within a national park. It assists in managing the tension between use and preservation.

The zoning system provides a means to ensure that the majority of national park lands and their living resources are protected in a wilderness state with a minimum of man-made facilities. Zones permitting a concentration of visitor activities and supporting facilities and services will occupy no more than a small proportion of lands in a national park. Moreover, in certain national parks in remote areas no provision will be made for such zones. In national parks where traditional uses are permitted, the park zoning plan will accommodate such activities.

2.1

The zoning system will reflect Parks Canada's policies and will facilitate their application in individual national parks.

2.2

The national park zoning system will apply to all land and water areas of national parks, and to other natural areas within the Parks Canada system as appropriate.

2.3

A zoning plan will be an integral part of each national park management plan.

2.4

The national park zoning system will consist of the following five zones:

2.4.1

Zone I - Special Preservation

Specific areas or features which deserve special preservation because they contain or support unique, rare or endangered features or the best examples of natural features. Access and use will be strictly controlled or may be prohibited altogether. No motorized access or man-made facilities will be permitted.

2.4.2

Zone II - Wilderness

Extensive areas which are good representations of each of the natural history themes of the park and which will be maintained in a wilderness state. Only certain activities requiring limited primitive visitor facilities appropriate to a wilderness experience will be allowed. Limits will be placed on numbers of users. No motorized access will be permitted. Management actions will ensure that visitors are dispersed.

2.4.3

Zone III - Natural Environment

Areas that are maintained as natural environments and which can sustain, with a minimum of impairment, a selected range of low-density outdoor activities with a minimum of related facilities. Non-motorized access will be preferred. Access by public transit will be permitted. Controlled access by private vehicles will only be permitted where it has traditionally been allowed in the past.

2.4.4

Zone IV - Outdoor Recreation

Limited areas that can accommodate a broad range of education, outdoor recreation opportunities and related facilities in ways that respect the natural landscape and that are safe and convenient. Motorized access will be permitted and may be separated from non-motorized access.

2.4.5

Zone V - Park Services

Towns and visitor centres in certain existing national parks which contain a concentration of visitor services and support facilities as well as park administration functions. Motorized access will be permitted.

3.0
Protecting National Park Resources

Land management within national parks differs markedly from that of most other lands, where effort is directed toward modifying or controlling nature, producing crops or extracting natural resources. Within national parks, effort is directed towards protecting our natural heritage by maintaining the physical environment in as natural a state as possible. This fact has far-reaching implications for the resource management of national parks in that many concepts or ideas which are relevant or essential to the successful management of other lands have limited relevance to the management of national parks. Therefore, caution should be exercised before any active manipulation of park resources is undertaken with preference given to allowing natural processes to function unless they have been clearly altered or made inoperative by man-induced changes.

The management of national parks should not, however, be in isolation from the regions in which they are located. Few, if any, land uses, either within or outside national parks, can occur without there being both beneficial and detrimental effects on the surrounding lands, Co-operation with other land management agencies is therefore essential.

National parks are special areas which are protected by federal legislation from all forms of extractive resource use such as mining, forestry, agriculture, oil, gas and hydro electric development and sport hunting. In some new national parks, however, certain traditional resource uses by local residents may be allowed to continue. Such activities must not destroy or seriously impair the natural values for which the park was established. They will be clearly agreed to in each case at the time of formal establishment of the national park. It is also essential that in establishing new national parks Parks Canada honour the treaties of Indian people which in some cases may involve hunting, fishing and trapping rights in national parks.

The natural and cultural resources of a national park must be protected from the effects of man's activities so that they can be left unimpaired for future generations. Actions by Parks Canada to provide for public understanding and enjoyment of national parks must be carefully considered to minimize their environmental impact. The process of environmental assessment and review is intended to ensure that the full-range of possible adverse effects of any action within national parks is identified, measured and evaluated and that measures are taken to reduce foreseen adverse impacts or to proceed with alternative actions.

3.1
Resource Protection

Natural resources within national parks will be given the highest degree of protection to ensure the perpetuation of a natural environment essentially unaltered by human activity.

3.2
Resource Management

3.2.1
Natural resources within national parks will be protected and managed with minimal interference to natural processes to ensure the perpetuation of naturally evolving land and water environments and their associated species.

3.2.2
An integrated natural resource data base will be developed and maintained for each national park.

3.2.3
Manipulation of naturally occurring processes such as fire, insects and disease may take place only after monitoring has shown that:
i)there may be serious adverse effects on neighbouring lands; or
ii)public health or safety is threatened; or
iii)major park facilities are threatened; or
iv)natural processes have been altered by man and manipulation is required to restore the natural balance; or
v)a major natural control is absent from the park; or
vi)the continued existence of a plant or animal species, which is rare or endangered or which is critical to representation of the natural region, is threatened by a natural cause such as insects or disease; or
vii)the population of an animal species or stage of plant succession which has been prescribed in the objectives for a park, cannot be maintained by natural forces.

3.2.4
Where active resource management is necessary, techniques will duplicate natural processes as closely as possible.

3.2.5
Resource management in each national park will take into account factors such as park size, objectives, zoning, geographic location and the nature of activities occurring in surrounding areas.

3.2.6
Habitat critical to the survival of an animal or plant species or population may be provided by

acquisition, agreement with other agencies or habitat manipulation within the park.

3.2.7
A species of plant or animal which has been native to, but which is no longer present in the park area, may be reintroduced:
i)if the effect on other plants and animals is acceptable; and
ii)if such action is compatible with park objectives; and
iii)if such action does not pose serious problems for neighbouring land uses.

3.2.8
Non native species of plants and animals will not be introduced into a national park and, where they exist, efforts will be made to remove them.

3.2.9
Parks Canada will seek to eliminate or minimize sources of pollution affecting park resources. Where sources of pollution are external to the park, Parks Canada will work in co-operation with other responsible agencies.

3.2.10
Commercial exploration, extraction or development of natural resources will not be permitted in a national park.

3.2.11
Certain traditional extractive activities will be permitted in the following circumstances:
i)In new national parks, guarantees will be provided so that certain traditional subsistence resource uses by local people will be permitted to continue in parts of national parks for one or more generations when such uses are an essential part of the local way of life and when no alternatives exist outside the park boundaries. These exceptions will be agreed to at the time of formal establishment of a new national park and will be outlined in the park management plan.
ii)Selected activities which are of cultural value in portraying to visitors traditional relationships between man and the land in the park area as part of the park experience may be permitted.
iii)In new national parks, the treaty rights of Indian people and those rights recognized in native land claims settlements will be honoured and extractive activities which are the subject of such rights can only be terminated after agreement has been reached with the people concerned.
iv)Controlled sport fishing of naturally regenerating populations of native species will be permitted.

All such activities will be subject to the requirement

to protect the ecosystems and maintain viable populations of fish and wildlife species.

3.2.12
Places of national historic significance within national parks will be protected and managed according to the policies of national historic sites or national historic parks.

3.2.13
Significant archaelogical resources in national parks will be protected.

3.2.14
Other historical and cultural resources within national parks will be protected:
i)when such resources are of particular significance and/or interest to the public; and
ii)when public use and access can be controlled so that significant natural values are not impaired.

3.3
Environmental Assessment and Review

3.3.1
All developments, plans and management activities occurring on national park lands, including those proposed by agencies other than Parks Canada, will be subject to an assessment and review process which ensures that the environmental implications are fully considered in decision-making.

3.3.2
The process used for environmental assessment and review within national parks will be consistent with the Federal Environmental Assessment and Review Process (E.A.R.P.).

3.3.3
All products of the environmental assessment and review process including screening reports, initial environmental evaluations and environmental impact statements will be available for public review.

4.0
Public Understanding, Appreciation and Enjoyment of National Parks
Canadians are encouraged to visit national parks and Parks Canada has a responsibility to provide opportunities for the public to enjoy and understand these special places in ways which are compatible with the long term protection of their natural values.

In responding to visitor needs for services, facilities and outdoor recreation activities, Parks Canada must act with care and imagination. All Canadians have a right to appreciate their natural heritage but the means of doing so and the facilities provided will depend on the sensitivity of the environment to human impact. National parks offer rare and outstanding opportunities to experience and learn about the natural environment in a wilderness setting. They cannot, however, provide for every kind of use requested by the public. Because national parks are dedicated to future as well as present generations, impairment by overuse, improper use and inappropriate development must be avoided. As a general guideline, simplicity in facilities and self-reliance on the part of visitors will be encouraged.

Parks Canada also has a responsibility to inform the Canadian public about their national parks and to provide programs which encourage a better understanding of these natural areas of Canadian significance. Co-operative action with the many agencies, groups and citizens concerned about national parks can supplement Parks Canada's own efforts to increase public awareness of national parks objectives and issues. In these ways, public support and wise use, which are necessary for continuing protection of national parks, may be achieved.

4.1
Visitor Use

4.1.1
Parks Canada will provide for a variety of outdoor recreation opportunities which are a means for park visitors to enjoy and understand the park's natural environment and which are consistent with the protection of park resources.

4.1.2
Parks Canada will provide for those outdoor recreation activities which are dependent upon a park's natural resources and require a minimum of man-made facilities.

4.1.3
Within the above constraints, provision will be made for activities in which visitors of diverse interests, ages and skills can participate throughout the year.

4.1.4
Parks Canada will encourage private sector and non-governmental organizations to provide skill development programs.

4.1.5
Parks Canada will regulate the amount, kind, time and location of outdoor recreation activities using the zoning plan and other management actions to protect park resources or to ensure visitor safety and enjoyment.

4.1.6
No new golf courses and downhill ski areas will be developed in national parks. Where downhill ski areas exist they will be permitted to develop to the capacity of their legislated boundaries.

4.2
Information and Interpretation

4.2.1
Accurate information about national parks will be made available to all Canadians as well as to park visitors so as to encourage and assist them to appreciate and enjoy national parks.

4.2.2
Parks Canada will provide information to make visitors aware of the opportunities for understanding, appreciation and enjoyment of a national park, such as programs, facilities and services available, relevant regulations and necessary skills and equipment.

4.2.3
Park Canada will present accurate on-site interpretation programs which will promote understanding and appreciation of the park's natural, cultural and historical values and which will develop an awareness of man's relationship to and dependence on the natural environment.

4.2.4
Parks Canada will provide information services and programs to educational institutions, public associations and to those providing public services in national parks so as to help promote awareness and wise use of national parks.

4.2.5
Parks Canada will develop co-operative arrangements with organizations and individuals to promote public appreciation and enjoyment of national parks and to encourage their protection.

4.2.6
Parks Canada will provide opportunities for individuals, private sector and non-governmental organizations to volunteer services in national parks.

4.3
Visitor Services and Facilities

4.3.1
Commercial services and facilities such as hotels, stores and service stations and park administration buildings will, wherever feasible, be located in communities adjacent to national parks.

4.3.2
Parks Canada will ensure that facilities and services essential for public understanding and enjoyment of national parks are provided within appropriate zones.

4.3.3
Essential facilities and services within national parks will normally be grouped together in visitor centres for public convenience, energy conservation and protection of park resources.

4.3.4
Parks Canada will encourage involvement of the private sector including non-government organizations in the development and operation of certain approved services and facilities for visitors in national parks.

4.3.5
All facilities and services in national parks will be maintained to suitable standards.

4.3.6
Rates charged to the public for the use of facilities and services provided either by Parks Canada or by private enterprise should be comparable to those outside national parks for similar services.

4.3.7
Where crafts are sold to the public Parks Canada will encourage the promotion of products made in Canada, particularly native handicrafts.

4.3.8
The scale, site, form and character of buildings within national parks will be as unobtrusive as possible so that park architecture is in harmony with the natural surroundings.

4.3.9
Park Access and Circulation

4.3.9.1
Access to and circulation within national parks will be encouraged so as to provide the public with the opportunity of understanding and enjoying the park in conformity with the zoning plan.

4.3.9.2
Non-motorized means of transportation will be used in national parks wherever feasible. Where motorized transportation is required, preference will be given to public transportation.

4.3.9.3
Air transportation will not be permitted within national parks except in strictly controlled circumstances. Efforts will be made to restrict aircraft to specific flight lines and altitudes.

4.3.9.4
New communication, transportation and utility corridors will not be routed through national parks.

4.3.10
Visitor Accommodation

4.3.10.1
Within national parks, preference will be given to basic accommodation facilities such as campgrounds, hostels and shelters which enhance visitors' appreciation and enjoyment of the parks' natural values.

4.3.10.2
Campgrounds and other forms of basic accommodation in national parks will be developed in ways which provide visitors with the greatest possible opportunity to experience the natural environment and require a minimum of support facilities and services.

4.3.10.3
In certain parks more substantial accommodation facilities may be provided because alternatives are too distant.

4.3.10.4
All commercial accommodation facilities within national parks will be available for use by the general public. National park lands will not be available for the development of new private cottages or camps.

4.3.10.5
Condominium ownership of visitor accommodation will not be permitted. Condominium ownership of accommodation for those who need to reside in existing park towns will be allowed.

4.3.11
Land Tenure

4.3.11.1
Limited tenure may be granted on national park lands in the form of leases, concessions or licenses of occupation for the provision of essential services and facilities for park visitors.

4.3.11.2
Holders of land tenure agreements for the use of national park lands will pay an economic rent.

4.3.11.3
Existing leasehold interests in national parks will be acquired if the lands or facilities are needed for public purposes.

4.3.12
National Park Towns
Because of their size, permanent population, year round services and extensive municipal infrastructure, Banff and Jasper are classified as national park towns. They are unique park communities which have the tax base necessary to support local self-government. Other developed areas, offering services to the public, are designated as visitor centres. These are defined as those planned areas in a park developed and managed to provide services and facilities.

4.3.12.1
Existing towns (Banff and Jasper) will be limited to the boundaries established by legislation.

4.3.12.2
No new towns will be developed within national parks.

4.3.12.3
Parks Canada will continue to own all land and administer land-use planning in national park towns.

4.3.12.4
The formation of local government to administer services and certain facilities will be encouraged.

4.3.13
Residency

4.3.13.1
Permanent residency in national parks will be limited to those who are providing essential services and who cannot reasonably live outside the park. Temporary residency will be permitted where it is necessary for approved traditional uses.

4.3.13.2
Permanent residents of national parks will live within a visitor centre or a town if such exists.

4.3.13.3
Parks Canada will levy charges on residents of visitor centres and towns, in cases where local government does not exist, to recover an equitable portion of the costs of developing and maintaining municipal services.

5.0
Research
Research is essential at all stages in the establishment, development and management of the national parks system. Parks Canada strives to learn about the natural environment so that national parks can be identified, protected and accurately interpreted to the public. In addition, research is important to assess public needs and the impact of visitor uses and facilities.

National parks also offer opportunities for basic scientific research. While such research may not be essential for park management it may expand man's fund of knowledge and enable parks to serve as benchmarks for ecological research and for studies of the effects of modern technology on lands outside park boundaries.

5.1
Parks Canada will encourage and conduct research into natural phenomena, public needs, visitor use and impacts so as to contribute directly to the identification, selection, establishment, protection, development, interpretation, planning and managing of national parks.

5.2
Other research in national parks which will enhance understanding of natural processes and/or enjoyment of natural areas will be authorized:
i) when use of a national park environment is essential; and
ii) when such research is undertaken or sponsored by a qualified individual or organization.

5.3
Research activities and facilities within national parks will be controlled by Parks Canada to protect natural resources.

5.4
Temporary research facilities may be located within national parks for the use of Parks Canada and to encourage compatible or complementary research by other agencies.

5.5
Parks Canada will co-operate with and draw upon the research of other government agencies, universities and non-governmental organizations and upon the knowledge of individual citizens.

5.6
Current research information will be made available to the public. Where appropriate, research activities will be demonstrated and interpreted to enhance public understanding of the natural environment.

6.0
Management Plans

A management plan is a guide, approved by the Minister, by which Parks Canada administers the resources and uses of a particular national park. Each plan is an expression of Parks Canada's policies for a national park within its regional context. As a public document, the plan provides information on the opportunities which are available to understand and enjoy the park and of the degree of protection which is necessary for different zones within the park.

The park management plan contains a statement of management objectives and the means and strategies for achieving them, stated in a broad but comprehensive manner. The level of detail is confined to the definition of the type, character, locale of developments, and the provision of guidelines for more detailed plans concerning resource management, interpretation and visitor use. The management plan is not an end in itself; rather it constitutes a framework within which subsequent management, implementation and detailed planning will take place. Zoning is a vital component of the management plan. Therefore, proposed changes to a zoning plan require public participation and ministerial approval.

Public participation at the national, regional and local levels is an essential part of the management planning process. A consistent general approach will be followed so as to involve the public from the early stages in key decisions including preparation of park objectives, formulation of alternative park concepts, selection of a final park management plan and any proposed major changes to the plan.

The policies in this document will guide Park Canada's actions in the future. There are however, certain developments in national parks which were permitted or even encouraged in the past but which would not be acceptable today. Such developments will not be allowed to expand and similar new ones will not be permitted. Ideally non-conforming developments should be removed, especially when they result in significant impairment. Often this will not be possible for a variety of reasons related to their long tradition of use. The future of particular non-conforming uses within individual national parks

will be decided after public consultation on the management plan for the park.

6.1
A management plan will be prepared for each national park as an expression of Parks Canada's policies and as a guide in park management.

6.2
The management plan will contain a statement of the approved park objectives which will reflect Parks Canada's objective for national parks, and the role of the park in the system of national parks and in the area in which it is located.

6.3
Opportunities will be provided for the Canadian public to be regularly involved from the early stages in the development of management plans for national parks including the preparation of park objectives, the formulation of alternative park concepts, the selection of the final park management plan and any proposed major changes to the plan.

6.4
The management plan and changes thereto must be approved by the Minister responsible for Parks Canada.

6.5
Parks Canada will continuously monitor the implementation of park management plans and will periodically undertake formal plan reviews.

6.6
Parks Canada will co-operate with other levels of government, private organizations and individuals responsible for the planning of areas adjacent to national parks and for the provision of facilities and services in adjacent communities to ensure that national parks are integrated in a positive manner with their surrounding regions.

6.7
In certain cases, financial assistance may be provided for the development of municipal infrastructure necessary to encourage tourism development outside national parks, by means of federal-provincial cost-sharing agreements through other federal agencies.

Figure 14:
The Steamer *Rideau King* leaving Chaffey's
Lock on the Rideau Canal, 1905

Courtesy of:
Mr. Neil Patterson, Kingston, Ontario.
A Pennock Photograph.

Background

In the early part of the last century, British North America embarked with great enthusiasm on a period of canal-building. Constructed prior to the development of railroads and highways, these early canals were intended to facilitate the flow of trade along waterways or, in some cases, to provide alternative routes in case of war. At Confederation the canals came under the jurisdiction of the federal government because of their importance in the transportation system of the new nation.

Since that time the role of these canals as commercial trading routes has diminished and, more recently, their use as recreational waterways has increased dramatically. In addition, the canals have taken on new significance as historic examples of early engineering technology in Canada and as scenic corridors.

In 1972, in recognition of these changes, the responsibility for certain canals was transferred from the Ministry of Transport to Parks Canada. The transfer was made on the understanding that future management of these canals would emphasize not only transportation but the protection, enjoyment and interpretation of their natural and cultural heritage values. The following heritage canals are now operated and maintained by Parks Canada: Rideau, Trent-Severn, Murray, Carillon, Ste. Anne, Chambly, St. Ours and St. Peters. These heritage canals are now an important part of the overall Parks Canada program.

Parks Canada Objective for Heritage Canals
To encourage public understanding and enjoyment of Canada's natural and cultural heritage by protecting for all time the heritage resources of certain federally operated canals and by operating these canals for recreational use.

1.0
Encouraging Public Understanding and Enjoyment
Heritage canals can provide a variety of opportunities for the public to enjoy recreational activities on land and water, and to appreciate aspects of Canada's natural and cultural heritage.

1.1
Information and interpretation programs will be developed by Parks Canada to provide canal users, visitors and the general public with an appreciation of the heritage values of each canal.

1.2
Parks Canada will ensure the provision of services and facilities which are essential to maintaining navigation routes, public land access, safety, enjoyment and understanding of heritage features.

1.3
A variety of compatible recreation activities will be encouraged so that the land and water resources of heritage canals can be used in all seasons wherever possible.

2.0
Protecting Heritage Resources
Heritage canals are navigation routes which include a variety of cultural, natural and recreational resources. Canals illustrate the evolution of man/land relationships and serve as a resource for contemporary recreational use.

2.1
Navigation along heritage canals will be maintained as an inherent part of their heritage value.

2.2
In the operation and maintenance of heritage canals and in the development of facilities and services for visitors, Parks Canada will protect the heritage character and original historic appearance of each canal. Exceptions may be approved under special circumstances for the mechanization of dams for the efficient control of water levels within the watershed.

2.3
Parks Canada will protect and interpret heritage resources which illustrate man's use of natural features for transportation, settlement or economic development.

2.4
Historic resources which have been identified as being of national historic significance will be protected according to the policies of National Historic Parks, while recognizing the special requirement for the maintenance of navigation.

2.5
Significant natural features on federal lands along heritage canal systems will be protected according to the policies of national landmarks.

2.6
Parks Canada may limit the level, type and location of use of heritage canals to protect heritage resources or to ensure visitor safety and enjoyment.

2.7
Canals will be maintained and operated in a manner that minimizes adverse effects on water quality and shoreline property.

3.0
Planning for Protection and Use of Heritage Canals
Parks Canada is responsible for the federally-owned heritage canals and associated lands. The development and management of each heritage canal and its associated lands should be based on a plan which provides for present and future use and ensures that the character of each heritage canal is protected.

Lands bordering canal waterways may be owned by provincial or municipal governments or by private owners. The planning for those areas which are exclusively federal responsibility must be closely co-ordinated with the planning of adjacent lands by other responsible agencies or individuals to ensure integration of canals with their environment.

3.1
Parks Canada will prepare plans to guide the development and management of those aspects of the heritage canals which are a federal responsibility.

3.2
Opportunities will be provided for the public to participate in the planning for heritage canals.

3.3
Parks Canada will co-operate with provincial and municipal governments as well as other groups and individuals responsible for the planning of lands adjacent to heritage canals; this will normally be accomplished through a co-operative agreement between the parties concerned.

Agreements for Recreation and Conservation

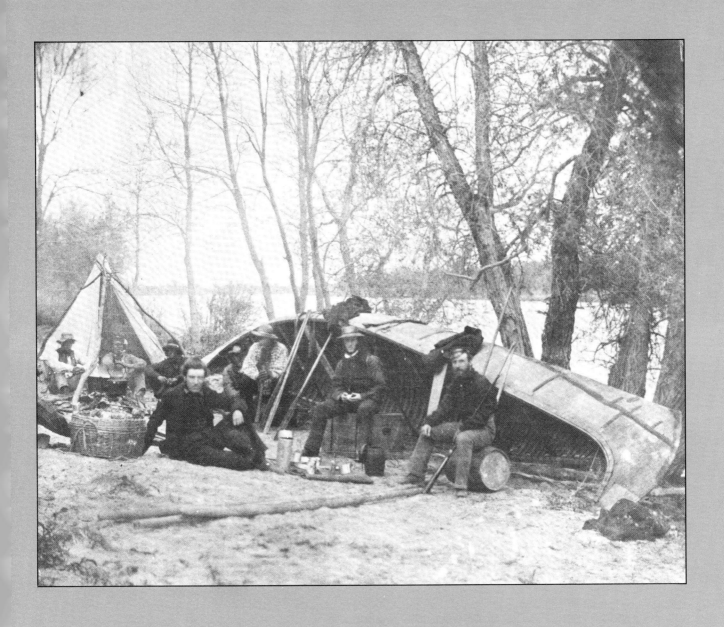

Figure 15:
Assiniboine and Saskatchewan Exploring Expedition.
Encampment of the H.Y. Hind party on the
banks of the Red River. June 1, 1858

Courtesy of:
The Public Archives of Canada
National Photography Collection
H.L. Hine Photographer

Background

Certain areas of natural and/or cultural heritage significance can best be protected and presented through the joint efforts of Parks Canada, provincial and territorial governments, other federal departments, other public and private organizations and individuals. Besides conservation and recreational significance, these areas generally have a substantial physical, economical and social impact on the region. The co-operative approach makes it possible to meet the objectives of the various participants through a joint agreement. Such agreements are called "Agreements for Recreation and Conservation" (ARC) and the areas they apply to are referred to as "co-operative heritage areas". This approach is broader in scope and can be more effective than unco-ordinated actions by individual agencies. It offers opportunities for heritage conservation, in circumstances where the less flexible national parks approach is unworkable because, for example, of extensive private ownership or ongoing resource extraction.

Co-operative heritage areas may be of several types. In some cases there may be a variety of distinctive natural and cultural resources concentrated in an area which, taken together, are of Canadian significance. In other cases there may be an example of one particular type of heritage resource which is considered to be of national significance, e.g., historic land and water routes, urban conservation areas or rural cultural landscapes, and whose preservation requires co-operative action. In identifying and selecting potential co-operative heritage areas, provinces and territories of course play a key role so that proposals reflect their priorities and responsibilities.

The first such agreement for recreation and conservation commits Canada and Ontario to joint planning in the corridor surrounding the Rideau and Trent-Severn canals. This agreement, signed in 1975, is known as the Canada-Ontario Rideau-Trent-Severn (CORTS) agreement. In addition, a Canada-Manitoba agreement was signed in 1978 for the joint development of the Red River Corridor north of Winnipeg, including historic, natural and recreational resources. Several other agreements are being discussed between Parks Canada and different provinces. While there are some similarities between these proposals, each one focuses on a particular combination of heritage resources and is designed to achieve the specific objectives of the participants.

Parks Canada Objective for Agreements for Recreation and Conservation
To protect significant natural and cultural resources within certain heritage areas and to encourage public use, understanding and recreational enjoyment of such areas by acting in conjunction with other governments, organizations and individuals through agreements for recreation and conservation.

1.0
Selecting Co-operative Heritage Areas
Co-operative heritage areas will be selected in co-operation with federal, provincial and territorial agencies and interested organizations and individuals. The selection of co-operative heritage areas will thus reflect provincial needs, for example in outdoor recreation, and be responsive to provincial programs and priorities. Parks Canada's assessment of potential co-operative heritage areas will be based on the following criteria:
i)Heritage Resources: The area will contain natural and/or cultural heritage resources which are of Canadian significance because of their quality and/or quantity; and
ii)Heritage Protection: The heritage resources will be in such condition and setting that continuing protection will be possible; and
iii)Need for Co-operation: The area will be such that the development of its heritage potential will require the participation and co-operation of other agencies with Parks Canada through agreement; and
iv)Agreement: It will be possible to accommodate the objectives and co-ordinate the independent actions of the participating agencies; and
v)Parks Canada System: The area will complement other elements in the Parks Canada system.

2.0
Joint Action
Agreements for recreation and conservation commit participating agencies to joint action in a process that involves research, planning, negotiation, development and management.

2.1
The agreement will clearly state the objectives and responsibilities of the participants.

2.2
The participants will jointly determine the strategy for the development and management of agreed activities by outlining the means of utilizing and integrating the authorities and resources of all participants.

2.3
Participating agencies will agree to undertake independently certain aspects of the agreed strategy.

2.4
New proposals for the protection and development of co-operative heritage areas will be evaluated in light of criteria and rationale by which the particular area was selected and the terms of the agreement.

2.5
Planning for a co-operative heritage area is a joint process which produces an integrated plan defining co-ordinated action.

2.6
Public participation in the planning process for co-operative heritage areas will be encouraged.

3.0
Protecting Heritage Resources

3.1
Natural and/or cultural heritage resources will be given appropriate protection by the participant who is responsible under the joint agreement.

3.2
National parks, national historic parks or canals within a co-operative heritage area will be administered by Parks Canada according to its policies for that particular activity.

3.3
Activities and uses will be controlled to protect heritage resources and to ensure public safety and enjoyment.

4.0
Encouraging Public Understanding and Recreational Use

4.1
Parks Canada's contribution in a co-operative heritage area will emphasize those information and interpretation programs, recreational activities, facilities and services which foster an appreciation and understanding of the heritage resources.

4.2
Depending on the nature of the co-operative heritage area, a wide range of uses and recreational activities will be encouraged to meet the objectives of the participants as stated in the joint agreement.

Part III
Policies for New
Parks Canada Initiatives

Canadian Landmarks
Canadian Heritage Rivers
Heritage Buildings

Figure 16:
St. Vincent St., Montreal, Quebec, n.d.

Courtesy of:
The Public Archives of Canada
National Photography Collection
Anonymous photographer.

Figure 17:
The Lower Falls of the Snake Indian River
in Jasper National Park, n.d.

Parks Canada Photo Library
Bill Oliver Photographer

Figure 18:
The Historic Properties of the
Halifax waterfront. November 1975

Indian and Northern Affairs
Engineering and Architecture Branch
Shawn MacKenzie Photographer

Figure 19:
Hoodoos, Banff National Park, n.d.

Parks Canada Photo Library
Bill Oliver Photographer

Figure 20:
Robert Bell's party in Camp,
Geographical Survey of Canada, 1887.

Courtesy of:
The Public Archives of Canada
National Photography Collection
Robert Bell Photographer.

16

17

19

18

20

Canadian Landmarks

Figure 21:
Hoodoos, Banff National Park, n.d.

Parks Canada Photo Library
Bill Oliver Photographer

Background

Throughout Canada there are many exceptional natural features and phenomena. They are an important part of our national heritage and should be protected for their educational and scientific value. Some natural wonders such as meteor impact craters, dinosaur fossil sites, subterranean caverns, volcanic cinder cones, glacial moraines and coral reefs cover only a small area and are found in isolation from national parks. Canadian landmarks are one means by which many of these significant natural values can be identified, interpreted and protected.

Landmarks differ from national parks in a number of respects. They are sites containing one or more unique, rare or exceptional natural features or phenomena of Canadian significance, rather than areas encompassing representative natural ecosystems. They are generally small in size compared to national parks. While like national parks they have high potential for public interest and appreciation, landmarks have particularly important scientific value. Because they are small and rare or unique in Canada, they can withstand less use than national parks. The nature and level of visitor use is more strictly controlled, with greater emphasis being given to educational activities. Research activities are encouraged provided they are compatible with the need to protect the natural values.

There are a variety of ways in which such exceptional natural sites can be protected. Parks Canada is proposing a flexible system of Canadian landmarks which could include sites owned and protected not only by Parks Canada but also by provincial governments or by others. The system of Canadian landmarks should strive to include all exceptional natural sites of Canadian significance. Such sites will be identified in consultation with provinces and territories for possible inclusion in this system of Canadian landmarks through studies of natural themes which are refinements of the following broad environmental categories: geology, landforms, vegetation, wildlife, climate, rivers and lakes, oceans and marine life. The criteria for selection of Canadian landmarks and the means by which they can be established and protected will be discussed and agreement sought with the provinces. The policies which follow the criteria will govern national landmarks under the jurisdiction of Parks Canada. These policies are intended to provide a basis for the inclusion of sites under the ownership and administration of other land managing agencies in the system of Canadian landmarks.

Parks Canada Objective for the Canadian Landmarks System

To foster protection for all time of exceptional natural sites of Canadian significance in a co-operative system of Canadian landmarks, and to encourage public understanding and appreciation of this natural heritage so as to leave it unimpaired for future generations.

1.0
Proposed Criteria for Inclusion in the Canadian Landmarks System

1.1
Canadian landmarks must be exceptional natural sites of Canadian significance identified according to the following criteria:
i)The sites must contain a natural feature or phenomenon which is unique or rare in Canada or the world, or the sites must be the best example of a particular natural theme component in Canada; and
ii)The sites must have experienced minimum modification by man or, if such modification has occurred, the main feature must be unaffected and the sites must have potential for restoration to a natural state.

1.2
Canadian landmarks will also satisfy the following criteria:
i)the sites will be of high scientific value and public interest; and
ii)the sites will be of a size and configuration so as to:
a) encompass a natural feature or phenomenon whose long-term protection is feasible; and
b) offer opportunities for research, public understanding and appreciation.

1.3
Consideration will also be given to:
i)the degree of protection or threats to the natural environment of the site; and
ii)competing land uses (recognizing, for example, the policy of the Department of Indian and Northern Affairs to ensure that an inventory of the non-renewable natural resource potential of areas in the Yukon and Northwest Territories be compiled prior to their formal establishment as landmarks); and
iii)geographic balance of national landmarks throughout Canada; and
iv)the location and objectives of other protected natural areas; and
v)appropriate international criteria.

1.4
In addition to meeting the above criteria before a site will be formally included in the Canadian

system, provision will be made for its long-term protection through legislation, regulations, policies and management plans.

Note
The following detailed policies will apply to national landmarks owned, protected and administered by Parks Canada as part of the system of Canadian landmarks.

2.0
Protecting National Landmark Resources
Within national landmarks, resource management will be directed primarily at the protection and preservation of a single natural feature or phenomenon. Manipulation may therefore be required when natural conditions threaten to alter or eradicate the protected feature or phenomenon.

2.1
Resource Protection
Natural resources within national landmarks will be protected under the National Parks Act to ensure the perpetuation of the main landmark feature or phenomenon.

2.2
Resource Management

2.2.1
Natural processes will normally be allowed to proceed without interference unless monitoring has shown that:
i) the main landmark feature or phenomenon is threatened; or
ii) there may be serious adverse effects on neighbouring lands; or
iii) public health or safety is threatened.

2.2.2
Surface or sub-surface extraction of natural resources from within a national landmark will not be permitted.

2.2.3
Subsurface extraction, from outside a national landmark, of natural resources located under the surface of the landmark will be permitted if the landmark will not be impaired as a result.

3.0
Public Understanding and Appreciation of National Landmarks
National landmarks will provide the public with unique opportunities to observe, learn about and appreciate Canada's natural heritage. Intensive use and development will not be appropriate at national landmarks because of their small size and unique

features. Local communities adjacent to landmarks will be encouraged to provide accommodation and food services.

3.1
Visitor Use

3.1.1
Parks Canada will provide for day-use activities which are a means for park visitors to appreciate and understand the unique natural sites and which are consistent with the protection of the landmark feature.

3.1.2
Interpretation, research and other educational uses will be encouraged at national landmarks.

3.1.3
Parks Canada will provide for those visitor activities which are dependent upon a landmark's natural resources and require a minimum of man-made facilities.

3.2
Visitor Services and Facilities

3.2.1
Parks Canada will ensure that those facilities and services essential for public understanding and appreciation of national landmarks are provided.

3.2.2
Controlled access will be provided if possible to the main landmark feature. This will, in most cases, be by public transit or walking trails.

3.2.3
Facility development at national landmarks will be restricted to that required for visitors' basic needs and for interpretation and study purposes.

3.3
Information and Interpretation

3.3.1
Accurate information about national landmarks and the opportunities which they provide will be made available to the general public.

3.3.2
Interpretive programs will be provided to encourage an appreciation and understanding of the landmark.

4.0
Research
National landmarks are exceptional sites of high

scientific value which offer excellent opportunities for research into natural features and processes. Management-oriented research will be also essential to identifying potential national landmarks and planning for their protection and for public appreciation.

4.1
Parks Canada will encourage and conduct research necessary to identify unique natural areas of Canadian significance and to select national landmark sites.

4.2
Parks Canada will encourage and conduct research at a national landmark which contributes to an understanding of natural features and processes and to planning and managing the national landmark.

4.3
Parks Canada will co-operate with and draw upon the research of other government agencies, universities, non-governmental organizations and the knowledge of individual citizens.

4.4
Research information will be made available to the public and where appropriate, research activities will be demonstrated and interpreted to enhance public understanding of the natural environment.

5.0
Management Plans
A management plan is a guide by which Parks Canada administers the resources and uses of a particular national landmark. It is an expression of Parks Canada's policies at the site level and, as a public document, it informs the public of the opportunities which are available to understand and appreciate the landmark and of the degree of protection which is necessary.

5.1
A management plan will be prepared for each national landmark as an expression of Parks Canada's policies and as a guide in the management of the site.

5.2
Opportunities will be provided for the Canadian public to participate in the planning of national landmarks.

5.3
The management plan and changes thereto must be approved by the Minister responsible for Parks Canada.

5.4
Parks Canada will co-operate with other levels of government, private organizations and individuals responsible for the planning of areas adjacent to national landmarks and for the provision of facilities and services in nearby communities to ensure that national landmarks are integrated in a positive manner into their surrounding regions.

Figure 22:
White water canoeing on the
Upper Natla River, July 1972

Parks Canada Photo Library
Wild River Survey
Anonymous Photographer

Background
In Canada we still have rivers that flow through essentially natural environments, their channels unobstructed and their waters relatively unpolluted. Such rivers are outstanding examples of our natural heritage. As well, some of these rivers provided a source of food and a means of transportation for native people and early settlers, thereby playing a significant role in the exploration, trade and settlement of our country. These rivers are important elements of Canada's natural and cultural heritage, which should be preserved in an unspoiled state for the benefit of present and future generations.

Concerns for preserving Canadian heritage rivers complement international efforts to protect significant elements of the world heritage. Canada, in fact, has heritage rivers in relative abundance as compared to other nations. Consequently, other nations would naturally look towards Canada to protect in perpetuity, some of the world's best examples.

Parks Canada's Wild Rivers Survey, conducted from 1971 to 1973, gathered information on approximately 16, 650 kilometres of rivers. The survey provided an opportunity for analyzing and comparing the scenic and recreational resources of major Canadian heritage rivers, and provides an opportunity to formulate goals for the preservation of the best examples of these rivers and their associated lands. The establishment of a Canadian heritage rivers system should be a long range program which intends to designate nationally significant environments in which rivers, unaltered by man, are the predominant features.

Parks Canada is proposing a system of Canadian heritage rivers which could include areas owned and protected by the federal, provincial or territorial governments. This policy outlines only draft criteria for the selection of heritage rivers to be included in such a Canadian system.

Parks Canada Objective for Canadian Heritage Rivers
To foster protection of outstanding examples of the major river environments of Canada in a co-operative system of Canadian heritage rivers, and to encourage public understanding and enjoyment of this natural heritage so as to leave it unimpaired for future generations.

Parks Canada's first actions to meet this objective will be to discuss and seek agreement with provinces and territories on the proposed criteria for inclusion in the system of Canadian Heritage Rivers, the process for establishing the system and the means for protecting and managing rivers or designated sectors of rivers of Canadian heritage significance.

Proposed Criteria for Inclusion in the Canadian Heritage Rivers System

1.Heritage rivers or designated sectors of rivers will be outstanding representations of the major river environments of Canada, with particular attention given to their role in Canadian history; and

2.Heritage rivers will satisfy the following physical criteria:
i)free of impoundments within designated sector; and
ii)shorelines essentially natural; and
iii)the water relatively free of man-made pollutants; and
iv)inaccessible by road except at occasional crossings; and
v)river flow sufficient to support low intensity recreation activities; and

3.Heritage rivers and their associated lands will exists as an environmental unit so as to:
i)provide visitors with a natural experience by preserving the lands seen from the river surface and the shorelines as much as possible in an unaltered state; and
ii)adequately portray the scale, character, and themes of the river regime and associated lands; and
iii)ensure the ecological integrity of the river and associated lands; and

4.Consideration will also be given to:
i)the degree of threat to the natural environment; and
ii)the geographic distribution of Canadian Heritage Rivers; and

5.In addition to meeting the above criteria, before a river will be formally included in the Canadian system, provision will be made for the long-term protection of heritage rivers through legislation, regulations, policies and management plans.

Heritage Buildings

Figure 23:
A photographer at Baie St. Paul,
Quebec 1929

Courtesy of:
The Public Archives of Canada
National Photography Collection
J.B. MacLaughlin Collection
Anonymous photographer.

Parks Canada's Objective for Heritage Buildings

To act as the coordinating federal agency in fostering the protection of Canada's architectural and cultural heritage through: the conservation of heritage buildings under federal jurisdiction; the elimination of disincentives to heritage building conservation; the development of cooperative programs with the provinces and territories to encourage public and private initiatives in this field.

Background

Heritage buildings are an important aspect of Canada's cultural heritage and the subject of increasing public and private interest. Not only is it important to protect the built environment as examples of Canada's architectural heritage but older buildings often enhance the quality of life in urban centres, they represent wise uses of energy and materials and assist tourism development. While recognizing the jurisdictional rights, responsibilities and priorities of provincial and municipal governments, Parks Canada can play an important role in coordinating federal initiatives in this field.

Firstly, the federal government can take steps to protect historic buildings it owns, to set an example for others. The heritage significance of certain federal buildings should be recognized and their protection and continued use assured.

Secondly, the federal government can review its legislation, policies and regulations with a view to eliminating, where practical, aspects which are disincentives to heritage building conservation. The federal Income Tax Act purportedly encourages demolition of older buildings under the provisions for terminal losses and recapture of depreciation. The National Building Code and Fire Regulations present other obstacles that discourage owners and builders from rehabilitating older structures as the costs involved in meeting specifications and standards can be prohibitive.

Thirdly the federal government can cooperate with the provinces and territories in developing programs of support and assistance in the rehabilitation of individual heritage buildings and of heritage areas or districts. The Canadian Inventory of Historic Building (CIHB), designed primarily to assist Parks Canada in the identification and evaluation of structures of national historic or architectural significance, serves as a source of basic information for all those who are interested in architectural history or conservation. A Canadian Register of Heritage Property (CRHP) program could be developed in cooperation with the provinces and territories along the lines originally proposed in 1977. This would provide a national register recognizing older buildings of architectural, cultural or historic merit based on nominations by an appropriate provincial or territorial committee.

The federal government is considering several possible ways to stimulate heritage building conservation in the private sector through the elimination of disincentives, the development of a special heritage building rehabilitation program through Central Mortgage and Housing Corporation and the possible introduction of tax incentives for owners of registered heritage buildings.

Taken together these federal actions could provide substantial impetus to heritage building conservation without infringing on provincial jurisdiction and responsibilities, or private sector initiatives. A federal policy should recognize the importance of heritage building conservation in all federal activities. Parks Canada will continue to play a lead role in encouraging and coordinating practical federal initiatives through the Federal Advisory and Coordinating Committee on Heritage Conservation (FACCHC).